Unique Pets

CHAMELEONS

Kristin Petrie
ABDO Publishing Company

visit us at
www.abdopublishing.com

Published by ABDO Publishing Company, PO Box 398166, Minneapolis, MN 55439.

Printed in the United States of America, North Mankato, Minnesota.
052012
092012

PRINTED ON RECYCLED PAPER

Cover Photo: Angi Nelson – www.reptilephotographer.co.uk
Interior Photos: Alamy p. 19; Corbis p. 10; Frans Lanting/National Geographic Stock p. 8; Getty Images pp. 4–5, 11, 14–15, 17; Ingo Arndt/Minden Pictures/National Geographic Stock p. 7; iStockphoto pp. 9, 13; Tim Laman/National Geographic Stock p. 7; ZSSD/Minden Pictures/National Geographic Stock p. 21

Series Coordinator: Megan M. Gunderson
Editors: Megan M. Gunderson, BreAnn Rumsch
Art Direction: Neil Klinepier

Library of Congress Cataloging-in-Publication Data

Petrie, Kristin, 1970-
Chameleons / Kristin Petrie.
p. cm. -- (Unique pets)
Includes index.
ISBN 978-1-61783-439-4
1. Chameleons as pets--Juvenile literature. I. Title.
SF459.C45P48 2013
639.3'95--dc23

2012004887

Thinking about a Unique Pet?
Some communities have laws that regulate the ownership of unique pets. Be sure to check with your local authorities before buying one of these special animals.

Contents

CHAMELEONS

What has bulging eyes, scaly skin, and a long, sticky tongue? It may also have horns on its head and spines down its back. Best of all, it can change colors! This mysterious creature is a chameleon, of course!

Like other lizards, chameleons belong to the class Reptilia. More than 150 species of chameleons make up the family Chamaeleonidae.

Why keep this prehistoric-looking creature as a pet? Chameleons are **unique**. Their slow, precise movements are captivating. They are sensitive and solitary, but entertaining. And who wouldn't want a pet that changes colors? That's pretty cool!

A chameleon can't change to match any background. It won't become striped if you put it on a striped pillow. Instead, each species has its own set of colors and patterns.

Where They Live

Chameleons are native to Africa, southern Asia, and southern Europe. Today, **feral** chameleons can also be found in Florida, Hawaii, and California.

To see the most chameleons in nature, you would need to visit Madagascar. This African island is crawling with chameleons! It is home to about half of the world's chameleon species.

Chameleons are primarily **arboreal**. So, most live in trees and bushes. But some live among the dead leaves of the forest floor.

Each chameleon species has adapted to survive in a particular **environment**. Some species live in the rain forest **canopy**, along rivers, on plantations, or even in areas with lots of people. Others live in **savannas**, grasslands, **humid** mountain forests, or even deserts.

Crested chameleons live in humid rain forests.

Namaqua chameleons live in the dry Namib desert.

DEFENSE

In the wild, chameleons make tasty meals for birds, snakes, and spiders. Luckily, their natural coloring acts as **camouflage**. And, their forest homes help keep them safe. Chameleons can drop to the ground to avoid predators. And, they will move to the far side of a branch to hide from danger.

Chameleons also work hard to defend their territory from other chameleons. Some puff up their bodies and throats to look bigger and tougher! Others

Chameleons rock back and forth between each step. So, predators may think they are just leaves blowing in the wind.

change colors or wave special head flaps. Or they may charge, whip their tails, or snap their jaws to scare off invaders.

Sadly, humans are the greatest threat to chameleons. Deforestation destroys the homes of many species. Capture for sale in the pet trade also puts the chameleon population in peril. So, some chameleon species are **endangered**.

A coiled tail makes a chameleon look larger and fiercer to enemies.

What They Look Like

To help stay hidden, most chameleons have the coloring of their natural surroundings. Their color varies by species, age, and geographic origin.

Chameleons also range greatly in size. A *Brookesia minima* can perch on your fingertip. It is less than one inch (2.5 cm) long! The much larger *Furcifer oustaleti* measures up to 23 inches (58 cm) in length.

Male Jackson's chameleons have three horns.

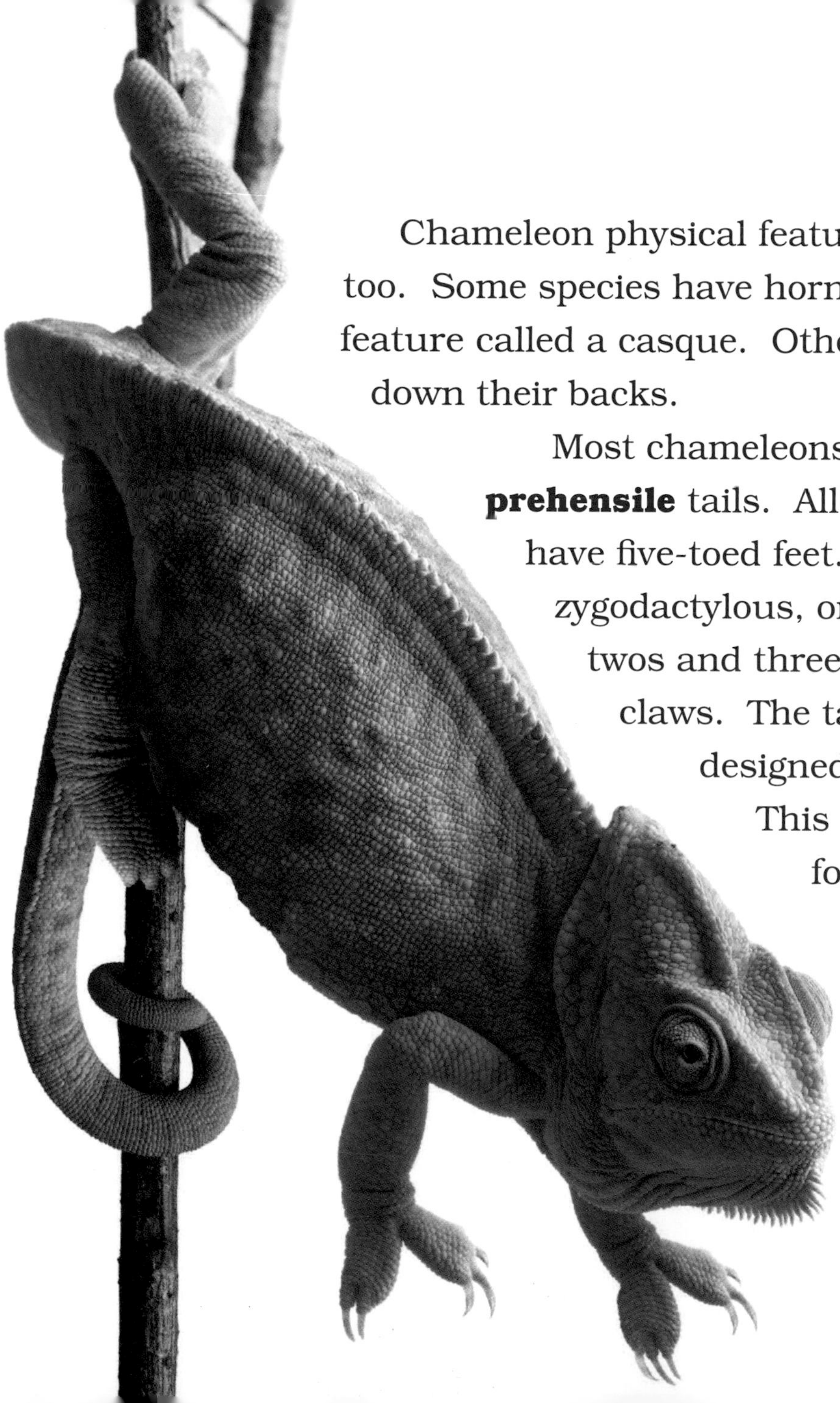

Chameleon physical features vary greatly, too. Some species have horns or a crown-like feature called a casque. Others have spines down their backs.

Most chameleons have **prehensile** tails. All chameleons have five-toed feet. The toes are zygodactylous, or grouped in twos and threes. They end in claws. The tail and toes are designed for grasping. This comes in handy for balance while climbing trees or snoozing on slim branches.

Behaviors

The chameleon's feet are great for more than just gripping. Their undersides are extremely sensitive. They tell the chameleon about the surface it is on.

Like a camera, the chameleon's special eyes can zoom in to see details from far away. Even more impressive, each eye can move independently. So, one eye can look forward while the other looks backward!

The chameleon's scaly skin also has important jobs to do. To keep the chameleon comfortable, it changes color in response to outside temperature and light. An overheated chameleon lightens in color. That way, it absorbs less heat from the sun. A chilly chameleon darkens to absorb more heat.

A chameleon also changes color to reflect its mood and health. It might show anger with spots and deep colors. A sick chameleon's colors may look dull. This is a clue to call the veterinarian!

Scaly, cone-shaped eyelids leave small, round openings for the pupils.

Food

What do chameleons eat? Bugs, bugs, and more bugs! Crickets, grasshoppers, and stick insects are just a few of their favorites. Larger species also go for small birds. Some even eat other chameleons!

Pet chameleons should be fed daily. But, they are known to be picky eaters. So, owners must provide a variety to keep them interested.

Chameleons are not the fastest movers in the world. So how do they catch those zippy insect meals? It's all in their long, lightning-fast tongues.

A chameleon's tongue has great aim and a sticky tip to grab prey. Once caught, prey is returned to the chameleon's strong jaws. Crunch, crunch, and down it goes!

In nature, chameleons drink water droplets that collect on leaves or their casques. Chameleons don't recognize still water as a drinking source. So, pet chameleons need drip systems or dishes of moving water.

A chameleon's tongue can spring out to twice its body length!

REPRODUCTION

When ready to mate, a male chameleon's skin turns bright colors. This vibrant display attracts a female. After mating, some chameleon species give birth to live babies. But most lay eggs.

To lay eggs, the female leaves the trees for the ground. There, she lays a clutch of eggs. She buries them in soil under a rock or leaves. The eggs hatch several months later. The exact length of time depends on the temperature and moisture around the eggs.

Newborn chameleons are independent from the moment they hatch. They look like tiny adults, but they are not as brightly colored. Luckily, their tongues are fully functioning. Zap! The newborn's first meal is easily caught.

The number of eggs depends on the mother's size. Small chameleons may lay just 2 eggs. Larger chameleons may lay up to 100!

Despite this early independence, young chameleons are fragile. So, pet chameleons should be older before they are purchased. This allows the **breeder** to care for them properly while they grow.

CARE

Keeping a pet chameleon happy and healthy can be challenging. Each of these territorial creatures needs its own cage. The cage must be tall enough to contain plants and branches. This allows your pet to climb, hunt, and hide as it would in nature.

Like all reptiles, chameleons are cold-blooded, or ectothermic. Their body temperature varies with the temperature around them. So, a pet chameleon's cage needs lights and heat for warmth. It also needs darkness and lower temperatures.

Owners must remember to turn the chameleon's lights on every morning and off every evening. This **mimics** the light and temperature changes of the chameleon's natural **environment**.

Caring for a pet chameleon also means providing the right food. These predators eat only live food. So in addition to caring for their chameleons, some owners also raise insects!

It is dangerous and even deadly for a chameleon to get too hot or too cold.

Things They Need

Keeping your pet chameleon healthy is one of the greatest challenges you'll face. These delicate creatures are at high risk of having numerous illnesses. They can have parasites, bacteria, viruses, and other issues.

Possibly the toughest part of caring for a chameleon is giving it space. Most do not like being held. Too much attention causes them **stress**. This leads to illness and sometimes death.

Trained **breeders** can advise new owners on the best chameleon for them. Some species are hardier and more easily maintained by humans. These well cared for chameleons live an average of three to eight years.

While chameleons are challenging pets, they are also rewarding. Their antics provide hours of enjoyment. And their color changes are one of a kind!

THE PET TRADE

Some chameleons are taken from their natural habitats to be sold as pets. Being captured in the wild isn't just stressful for these tiny lizards. It can also harm the natural population. So before you purchase a chameleon, do your research so you can do what's right. Never buy an endangered species. And, try to purchase chameleons that have been bred in captivity.

Few veterinarians are trained in chameleon care. Locate an expert through the Association of Reptilian and Amphibian Veterinarians before purchasing your pet. And make sure the chameleon you want doesn't look like it already needs a trip to the vet. It should be healthy! Then you're off to a great start.

Glossary

arboreal (ahr-BAWR-ee-uhl) - living in or frequenting trees.

breeder - a person who raises animals.

camouflage - a disguise or way of hiding something by covering it up or changing its appearance.

canopy - the uppermost spreading, branchy layer of a forest.

endangered - in danger of becoming extinct.

environment - all the surroundings that affect the growth and well-being of a living thing.

feral (FIHR-uhl) - having gone back to the original wild or untamed state after being tame.

humid - having moisture or dampness in the air.

mimic - to imitate or copy.

prehensile - adapted for grasping or holding. Some monkeys and other animals have prehensile tails.

savanna - a grassy plain with few or no trees.

stress - a physical, chemical, or emotional factor that causes bodily or mental strain.

unique - being the only one of its kind.

Web Sites

To learn more about chameleons, visit ABDO Publishing Company online. Web sites about chameleons are featured on our Book Links page. These links are routinely monitored and updated to provide the most current information available.

www.abdopublishing.com

INDEX